THE UNMERCIFUL PAIN

Madison Esther Panti

ISBN 978-1-68526-222-8 (Paperback)
ISBN 978-1-68526-224-2 (Hardcover)
ISBN 978-1-68526-223-5 (Digital)

Covenant Books
11661 Hwy 707
Murrells Inlet, SC 29576
www.covenantbooks.com

Truly he is my rock and my salvation; he is
my fortress, I will not be shaken.

—Psalms 62:6 NIV

ACKNOWLEDGMENT

I would like to thank God for the strength, grace, and mercy that He showered upon me during the time I felt so broken with an illness that had started to make me lose hope.

But God always reminded me of Isaiah 41:10 (NIV):

> Do not fear, for I am with you; do not be dismayed, for I am your God. I will strengthen you and help you; I will uphold you with my righteous right hand.

A big "Thank you" to Joana, Leonard, Eric, Poku, Ronald, Rebecca, Ada, Sylvia, Kwaku, Akua, Obi, Nana, Doris, Kofi, Rev. Dr. John Aneimeke and the BCAG congregation, Alex, Paulin, Mia, Philo, Dora, and so many others; I can't thank you all enough for the affection, support, prayers, encouragement, the rides to doctors appointments, and much more.

The Lord bless you and keep you! May the Lord make His face shine upon you and all your generations to come!

CHAPTER 1

It was a blissful Tuesday morning in the month of February 2021. The sun was out, yet it was very cold, but that did not stop the birds outside from singing. Even though we do not understand the songs, they're so comforting to the mind, soul, and body. It was, as usual, a glorious morning, as I started to get ready for my daily activities, like walking, driving to the shopping stores, and a few other chores here and there, before getting ready for work. As I sat on my bed in the morning, which was my usual routine of doing a few stretches before getting up completely, I started feeling a pinching pain in my right thigh. As I was not in pain the previous day, I thought it was a muscle spasm and went about my daily activities for the day after taking two over-the-counter ibuprofen tablets.

The day went on smoothly with no issues at all; the pain literally disappeared, so as usual, I was excited to go see my second family members at work in the evening, which was my regular shift. About thirty minutes into the shift, which requires sitting or standing sometimes, I started feeling a pinching, crushing, piercing, severe torture going down my right thigh and right leg.

I called Susan, my supervisor, right away to let her know my current condition. "I am not feeling well, looks like I am experiencing some severe pain in my right thigh, and the pain is going down my right leg," I said.

Susan responded, "Oh my gosh, Abigail, I am so sorry to hear that. I suggest you go home right away and please take care of yourself. Also update me of any developments, okay? You will be in my thoughts and prayers."

"Thank you so much, Susan. Good night," I said.

I left work to go back home with difficulty driving, but fortunately, the distance from work to the house was not very far. I took two more of the ibuprofen tablets and slept on the floor, with the hope that I would feel much better by the next morning. I was able to fall asleep, and by six o'clock in the morning, I woke up with a crushing, squeezing, horrible, pinching pain in my right thigh and my right leg. I couldn't get myself up off the floor. Everything was happening so fast; I felt my world and my life were crashing down. This experience was worse than giving birth naturally. Wow, obviously, something was wrong; my right thigh and my right leg were sending me signals for some emergency care that needed to be attended to almost immediately, which reminded me of when those red flags on your car's dashboard started to blink warning signs.

CHAPTER 2

This was getting serious, I thought, and immediately started getting ready to go to Agape Emergency Room as it was too early to call my primary doctor's office. Driving to the emergency room was another tough experience because the pain had become so excruciating like a knife cutting into my flesh. I felt a burning sensation caused by a movement. I felt my nerves moving from one location to another, pulling tightly, almost like being strangled or being held tight by my own nerves. The degree of total discomfort was unimaginable. There were times when I thought I would faint behind the wheel, and that scared me greatly. I began to regret not calling the ambulance. Then again, the exorbitant cost of a thirteen-minute ride in a bumpy, uncomfortable, and pain-reinforcing ride helped me to concentrate on the road ahead rather than the overriding pain in my thigh and my leg. I live about only thirteen minutes from Agape Emergency Room, but it would cost me roughly $1,200 or more, and that would be after my health-care insurance provider satisfies their part. So as slowly as a tortoise would, I managed to get to Agape Emergency Room.

Shirley, at the front desk, greeted me with a smile. I wanted to smile back at her, but at this point, I knew smiling back was not an option.

Shirley said, "Hi, good morning! What brings you in today?" I looked at Shirley with the perfectly painted smile and calm demeanor. I bet Shirley had seen lots of traumas in her career in the medical field, so my pain and my presence represented yet another day in a long line of trauma-sounding days. Yet another John Doe or whoever needing medical attention.

I wasn't anybody special. Somehow, that thought ripped my heart apart, and before I could control myself, large drops of tears began to slide down my cheeks. It choked me so hard that though I was in pain, I couldn't get the words out. It took some seconds before I could swallow hard enough to explain my presence. I finally looked at Shirley, and there she was, trying to look concerned and caring. Just maybe, things were not as bad as I felt. The pain didn't subside, but my crying did now.

Shirley was ready to help, but she also had to have me fill out paperwork and answer routine questions. In my mind, I was thinking, if only Shirley would show some empathy and get an override from her boss or someone in higher authority to let me complete the paperwork after seeing the doctor, as I could not even stand on my feet, let alone sit down. My body was bent for support with my left hand holding on to the counter where Shirley sat behind.

Shirley said, "Ms. Anderson, please fill all the questionnaire and, also, if I can get your ID and health insurance card." Her routine needs took precedence over my pain and discomfort. In my mind, I'm thinking, "Oh, Shirley, you don't understand my pain, but I guess it's not your fault, this is what you're trained to do and, I get it—it's the hospital's policy. But then again, I was thinking, so what about the patients who were involved in serious accidents and might not have any information on them at the time of trauma and admissions?

I guess there may be special codes to use for such cases, and I was not one of those special cases, so I worked through the pain and completed all the questions and all the paperwork on the clipboard.

CHAPTER 3

Shirley collected all the information and, with extreme efficiency, entered my insurance details into the computer. She then smiled, and for the first time, I noticed the glint of steel behind her eyes as she explained that based on my insurance I would need to make a payment of $500 as a copay. I had been in emergency rooms before and knew what that look represented. If you didn't pay, you would see the doctor for ten seconds, just enough time for him to tell you to go buy over-the-counter ibuprofen and not waste anybody's time. They couldn't exactly turn you away because you didn't have the money. They just spent a miniscule amount of time and essentially turned you away without explicitly stating it. I looked at her with a steady glint of my own. I took out my credit card and handed it to her. The steel cage behind her eyes disappeared once the payment was confirmed. The painted, fixed smile was back on her face. Business, as usual.

Dr. Johnson and Nurse Pat were nice and very approachable. Dr. Johnson asked me questions in a soothing tone while Nurse Pat smiled sympathetically and nodded as needed. Dr. Johnson administered a steroid injection and right away told me he suspected a lower-back pain caused by a nerve called the sciatic nerve. It was, apparently, pinching my nerves from my back and transferring the pain to my right thigh and my right leg. Oh wow! Never would have thought of how God designed our body's mechanism that pain in your thigh and your leg could be caused from the lower back. He is God all by himself, and His ways are many and not always easy to understand. Obviously, what a master planner God is!

The explanation of the cause of the pain sounded like music to my ears. "What, Doctor? What is that?" At this point, I had a thousand questions just circling in my brain, like "How did this happen?" "What was I going to do?" "How long was this going to take to heal?" "Tell me something, Doctor. I am all ears to listen to options, medications, or whatever it takes to heal me."

Dr. Johnson recommended a follow-up visit to my primary doctor as soon as possible and a release-paperwork instruction to see a specialist as soon as possible.

Pat came in and said she had experienced a similar situation, and showed me some exercises to do. What she didn't explain was that they didn't work! It didn't help me in the days ahead with my specific pain, even though they were great exercises.

So for less than two hours of emergency-room care, I paid $500 as copay, and I was sure other bills would welcome me in the mailbox somewhere down the line. *Wow* was all my mind was wavering at.

CHAPTER 4

I called Health First Medical Clinic to set up an appointment on that same day and had a date scheduled in three days' time after the emergency-room visit. That was the earliest available opening to have me go in for further evaluation. It was tough waiting for the days to pass by quickly, as the steroid injection administered at Agape Emergency Room was nothing but a waste of money and time because the torment of the pain did not subside for even a second. That was disappointing, thinking of that much money spent, not including what would be billed later for less than a two-hour visit.

I also notified my manager, Susan, about what was going on.

I have been a patient at Dr. Davis's clinic for about four years and have built a long-lasting relationship with almost everyone who works there.

As always, the staff were happy to see me for my routine checkups and always showed lots of empathy and support when I wasn't feeling well. Rose, one of the nurse assistants, whom I always referred to as my favorite, would always say these words to me, "Now you take care of yourself, Ms. Anderson," and I would respond, "Yes, Mommy." We both would laugh out loud. It's a blessing to share such cordial memories with people who are not even your family members.

Now when I walked into the clinic, literally struggling to balance myself, the employees knew right away something was terribly wrong. The staff didn't hear that vibrant voice from the patient they had established a family relationship with for so long.

I was bombarded with some of the curious questions I had during my visit to Agape Emergency Room, when I met with Dr. Johnson.

Their guesses were as good as mine, but at least I had an idea of what might be the root cause of this dreary thorn in my flesh.

Patricia, a nurse practitioner who attended to me, always came into the room and, as always, with a big smile, greeted me and asked the million-dollar question, "What brings you in today, Ms. Anderson? Looks like you're in pain. I didn't see that contagious smile of yours, so I am thinking you must be in lots of pain."

I mentioned to Patricia what Dr. Johnson had said would be the root cause of the pain and that he recommended seeing a specialist as soon as possible, but Patricia had a different opinion, that it was more of a muscle spasm, even though she had also received the same information about the diagnosis from Agape Emergency Room.

So at this point, there were two possibilities of the lower spine pinching nerves with miserable signals transferring all this unimaginable, disgusting pain down my right thigh and right leg or of a muscle spasm.

Patricia prescribed these medications for me to take: gabapentin, 300 milligrams; hydrocodone, 5 milligrams; acetaminophen, 325 milligrams; cyclobenzaprine, 10 milligrams; lisinopril, 20 milligrams; hydrochlorothiazide, 12.5 milligrams; and celecoxib, 100 milligrams (which I found out after five months of taking was a generic name for Celebrex, a blood thinner that caused my surgeon to cancel the long-awaited surgery in July 2021, due to possibilities of bleeding). That was very disappointing, but in all things, we give thanks to God, the author and finisher of our faith.

All these medications seemed awfully a lot to swallow on a daily basis, and I prayed they all worked, as I started feeling nervous, by reading the instructions and the adverse complications, about the side effects each medication might have.

I vividly remember back in the days growing up: whenever I was sick of fever or headaches, my grandmother would boil leaves, pour the leaves and the boiled water steaming hot into a bucket, had me sit down, and covered me up with a thick blanket for about five minutes intermittently until the vapor was all out. This process was repeated for three days, and after that, here I was jumping on my feet and fit as a fiddle.

Growing up, I occasionally visited my aunt Georgina, affectionately called George, as she preferred. Aunt George had a beautiful smile and would always make anyone around her laugh with jokes, which were so hilarious and contagious. I was walking down the street with Aunt George one evening in the year 1980, and she started talking about their father, who was my grandfather. She said her father, of blessed memory, was an herbalist in the 1930s and healed hundreds of sick people mainly from cuts, bruises, fractures from serious accidents, you name it. She mentioned how she witnessed a man who had a car accident and was taken to her father for healing. She mentioned how there was blood gushing out rapidly at an intermittent rate in a spray-jet manner (coinciding with the pulse) rather than the slower-but-steady flow of venous bleeding out everywhere, from broken bones to open flesh. She said her father started his mixtures of herbs and would send her to go bring this and that herb, mentioning the names. Hopping with joy just to be of assistance and be a part of saving the man's life, she would run to a room and bring the herbs as quickly as possible. Even at that tender age, she would pray quietly to God for the man to be healed. She said the man lived with them for about three months and was ready to go home, unlike in today's world, in which a person would be discharged from a hospital. He was walking like nothing had ever happened to him. She mentioned how their house had become a place to heal the sick.

As Patricia was still trying to figure out what the diagnosis would be for the torturing trauma with me, she referred me to see a physical therapist.

I notified Susan, my immediate manager at work, of progress reports. As always, a compassionate person. Susan said, "Oh, Abigail, I am sorry you have to go through this, but I will notify human resources of the new developments of your condition. Take care."

"I appreciate you," I said.

Amazing Moments

CHAPTER 5

I called the physical-therapy office to schedule an appointment, which I looked forward to, because whatever would make the pain go away was my main goal and focus right now.

In February 2021, which was my first session at Wellness Physical Therapy, I was greeted by Veronica at the reception desk. She was very welcoming and pleasant to talk to. I bet she knew most of the reasons we needed these therapies and really put herself in one's shoes, from what I experienced just interacting with her.

Veronica told me to have a seat and that Henry would be with me shortly. I said, "Oh, thank you, but I have not sat comfortably on a chair for weeks."

"Wow, that's crazy, and I can only imagine how that feels," said Veronica. "Thank you," I responded, and I walked away from the service window so she could continue with her work.

Not long after that, a gentleman called out my name and introduced himself as Henry, who would be doing some sessions with me to help with the suffering. "I look forward to that, Henry, and it's nice to meet you," I said.

Henry led the way to a big hall with lots of different exercise equipment. He asked some general questions, like if I was involved in any auto accident, and my response was no. So I told Henry what I had experienced, and he responded with good wishes of helping to get me back on my feet. What he didn't explain was that the exercises could intensify the pain.

Henry went over a printed sheet of my goals of sessions, starting from February 2021 to March 2021.

During the therapy, there were some exercises that were very uncomfortable and hurt like a double-edged sword piercing through my flesh and bones, so Henry would let me stop and say "Let's try this or that."

The first session lasted about thirty minutes. As much as it was difficult driving to the appointment, it got worse as I drove back to the house. As soon as I got home, I found myself on the floor, on my stomach, pouring out tears. I was hurting so bad I felt like puking. I was sicker to my stomach, and my whole body was fainting from all the shivering and shaking slightly and uncontrollably, as I was feeling cold and so frightened.

Oh, goodness! My right thigh felt like a double-edged sword had been pierced into it with severe burning, tingling, and throbbing. Tears were running down my cheeks, as if I were a child who had been grounded from playing with her favorite toy. Something was wrong. I had been in pain almost every day since early February, but this pinching, exertion, affliction, and piercing experience were an unmerciful pain.

I called the office right away, and even while I was speaking, I was in tears and choking on my saliva.

Henry got on the phone right away, showing concern and empathy in his voice, and advised me not to do the exercises he printed out as homework and that, on my next appointment, we would try something different. I appreciated his kind words. I emailed Health First Medical Clinic and updated Patricia on what had transpired at Wellness Physical Therapy.

The word *try* started ringing a bell in my ears again, as I had heard that from Patricia multiple times and Henry, as well. All the medications and exercises were not guaranteed to heal me. Just some trial-and-error practice that I had to pay a price for. That was inconceivable!

I was not looking forward to my next appointment session of the physical therapy, to tell you the truth.

I walked into the office, feeling as nervous as a cat with a long tail, in a room full of rocking chairs. Henry checked me in and said we would try a different exercise, as he had mentioned before. It didn't go too well, and Henry did let me know that some patients tolerated physical therapy well and others didn't. I wish that information had been disclosed to me before subjecting me to all the worst pain, which I knew was not intentional. So I guess I was one of the unlucky patients.

I was not able to continue my assigned exercises for the second time at home.

As the days passed by, I started hoping against hope as all odds seemed to be against me.

I had no choice but to call Wellness Physical Therapy and cancel my next appointment session, as I didn't want to put myself in danger after I recapitulated the unpleasant past experiences. I didn't get the chance to talk to Henry, as he was with a patient.

"Ms. Anderson, I understand you would like to cancel your remaining sessions due to the intensity of the pain, right?" Henry asked after he called me.

"Yes, Henry, that's right. I was very upbeat and enthused to go through these sessions, thinking I had found a safe haven, but unfortunately, the experience had been very scary, unpleasant, and unexpected, with the pain getting worse than I imagined," I said.

"That's understandable, Ms. Anderson. I would feel the same way. However, we would keep your file open. If anything changes and you decide to continue with the sessions, then please do not hesitate to give us a call. As always, thank you for choosing Wellness Physical Therapy," Henry said.

"I would definitely keep that in mind, Henry. Have a blessed day." I ended the call.

CHAPTER 6

After my visit to Agape Emergency Room; all the medications prescribed at Health First Medical Clinic, which I was still taking religiously with no promising effectiveness of healing; and the physical therapy, which had worsened my condition, I started feeling very hopeless but managed to keep a positive attitude and always would look at myself in the mirror with these words: "It shall be well" and "This, too, shall pass. God is not done with me yet." As I lay down on the bed, this old but powerful, promising song flashed through my memory:

> When we walk with the Lord in the light of His Word, what a glory He sheds on our way! While we do His good will, He abides with us still, and with all who will trust and obey. Trust and obey, for there's no other way to be happy in Jesus, but to trust and obey. Not a shadow can rise, not a cloud in the skies, but His smile quickly drives it away. Not a doubt or a fear, not a sigh or a tear, can abide while we trust and obey.

The Lord visited me one day in May 2021 as I lay down and I heard a voice say "Write a book about your life." I said "That is a long story," but I heard the voice say again, "Write this book about how this journey of the unmerciful pain started."

I gave excuses that I had never written a book and I couldn't even sit down. The Lord referred me to Exodus 4:10–12 (NIV):

> Moses said to the Lord, "Pardon your servant, Lord. I have never been eloquent, neither

in the past nor since you have spoken to your servant. I am slow of speech and tongue."

The Lord said to him, "Who gave human beings their mouths? Who makes them deaf or mute? Who gives them sight or makes them blind? Is It not I, the Lord? Now go; I will help you speak and will teach you what to say."

So I started the journey with me lying on the floor and wrote on the Samsung Notes app on my cell phone. On some days, I wrote two lines, and I was tired and in pain. On some days, I would go the extra mile and type a whole chapter.

The journey was tough when I couldn't sit comfortably to write, but I never gave up. I did it one day at a time, and I said to the Lord, as in *Psalm 19:14, "Let the words of my mouth and the meditation of my heart be acceptable in your sight, O Lord, my rock and my redeemer."*

So the journey went on and on till the end.

When you have gotten to ground zero of your life, never forget your creator! God was my only strong tower, whom I held on to. It didn't matter—all the phone calls, visits, and words of encouragement. Once you're all by yourself in that quiet moment, there's always that inner voice that speaks as softly as a summer breeze to your ears.

Somehow, I started thinking again of Dr. Johnson at Agape Emergency Room.

He had made a good point that the pinching nerves had to do with sciatica, so why didn't Patricia refer me to a specialist right away after? Dr. Johnson's instructions in the release paperwork to Health First Medical Clinic stated the need to see one as soon as possible, including a physical therapist. At least she referred me to a physical therapist, but that didn't help because the actual root cause of the sciatica had not been resolved yet.

CHAPTER 7

Crawling on the floor for months just to help myself to hold on to something solid to slowly get up had become a new lifestyle. To sit on the commode to urinate or eliminate feces meant tilting my buttocks, and I dreaded the fear of pushing out the feces as it felt like an electrical move and force in my body, as if I were being struck by lightning. It was so intense that my eyes would be bulging out with tears even though the feces were as soft as could be. The bulging disks were so painful that the slightest move could trigger the torture for hours on end.

It really made me rethink about life and all the little things that we take for granted.

For months, eating had become a norm of standing up or kneeling on my left leg on a chair; as sitting down triggered the pinching nerves. Eventually, it was so uncomfortable to do anything.

It reminded me of back in the days when I was young and very vibrant, life was full of parties, picnics, the beaches, long drives without feeling exhausted. Every step had to be brisk. Just rocking and rolling throughout the day without feeling worn out. Before I lay down to rest almost every night, I had the next day's activities all planned and laid out. I was an early bird and the last person to go to sleep. I could be on my feet all day and still had enough energy to do other chores while everyone else was asleep. As the years dawned on me, I started understanding the beauty of growing old, and I would be grounded at some point or another. All the youthful years started to wither away. I didn't have the desire to discuss some of the things I was so passionate about. I realized that even though I had all the freedom to do more as a grown-up than I would have in my youthful years, I rather saw most of the things I craved the most as vanity.

Now I couldn't even stand on my feet up to two hours without seeing my right foot swelling up and tingling in my right leg and under the foot. Then my right thigh and the nerves would start to hurt, triggering severe headaches that felt like rocks were falling on me. I thought it was interesting how sometimes the discomfort of the nerves moving at a violent and intense speed started from the right thigh to the right leg, to under the right foot, and sometimes vice versa. My only way of getting temporary relief was to lie flat on my stomach for roughly one hour or more or lie on my back for almost two hours and be as still as a statue.

CHAPTER 8

One night in March 2021, I was in severe pain that I sent a message to Health First Medical Clinic, pouring out my heart as to the continuous intensity of this wild, angry fire burning in my flesh, bones, veins, and nerves, so bad that I had lost complete trust in the crew of medical professionals I had known for years. I didn't think they were doing enough to rectify my concerns.

Where do I go from here to there? I felt like there was no other option, as my doctor seemed hesitant to refer me to another facility that could offer a deeper evaluation. When does one's concerns and frustrations become too much to be considered for a referral to another physician? That feeling of "I can't do this anymore" hit me real hard.

It was during these crucial moments when I prayed and asked God to have mercy on me. Then I remembered the simple but powerful words that my inner spirit always spoke softly to me about, "It shall be well." My faith in God became stronger and not wavering at all as I remembered Jeremiah 29:11:

> For I know the plans I have for you," declares the LORD, "plans to prosper you and not to harm you, plans to give you hope and a future.

And this song:

> He knows my name. Yes, he knows my name. And oh, how he walks with me. Yes oh,

how he talks with me. And oh, how he tells me
that I am his own.

The Bible verse Deuteronomy 31:6, "Be strong and courageous.
Do not be afraid or terrified because of them, for the LORD your
God goes with you; he will never leave you or forsake you" crossed
my mind like a flying eagle soaring high above the skies.

Those words became my pillar of hope, support, trust, encouragement, and healing.

Patricia at Health First Medical Clinic was good at responding
to messages, so she asked me if I could go in for an evaluation. As the
office was close by the house, I managed to drive slowly there, feeling
like the 1989 movie *Driving Miss Daisy*.

Crucial Pain Days

CHAPTER 9

Patricia, the nurse practitioner, decided that she would refer me to see a pain-management specialist for further evaluation and recommendations. At long last! After I endured the crushing, severe pain like a raging tsunami, Patricia had finally deemed it necessary for a referral to see Dr. Sam, so I immediately booked an appointment. The long-awaited time to get another opinion and a medical solution had arrived. It was not until thirty-nine days after the emergency room visit that Dr. Sam became my new pain-management specialist, after all odds had failed at Health First Medical Clinic and Wellness Physical Therapy. I had to endure the hustling and bustling of taking all those medications, none of which were effective, and the thought of that made me sicker every day.

I received the necessary new-patient paperwork via email; thank goodness for emails, and as you would imagine, it was a whole book of questionnaires to answer, but I was ready to provide every detailed information to get to the bottom of this ordeal.

I arrived at Dr. Sam's office on the second week of March 2021, and it was the closest of all the doctors' offices I went to, literally a walking distance from the house, so I couldn't be happier. Somehow, it was one of my worst days, as the torment of the pulling, crushing, excruciating experience of nagging torture in my flesh was just unbearable. My good friend Ebony was kind enough to drive me to the appointment.

I was ushered to a room after all verifications had been completed. As I couldn't sit, I knelt my left leg on a chair and waited for Dr. Sam. About twenty minutes passed, and there was no sign of Dr. Sam. After about thirty minutes, Angie came in and asked me some general questions while typing. Then I said the pain was very intense, and Angie said the doctor would be with me shortly, and without showing any empathy, she left the room. Angie might have been having a bad day or might have heard similar complaints from patients over and over. So I guess my situation wasn't any different for her to waste precious time to make any comment to me.

The nagging torture was getting worse, but I said to myself, "I was in good hands, so just be patient."

Finally, Dr. Sam came in. "Hi, my name is Dr. Sam, what brings you in today?" I guess it was routine questions. He looked very serious, and I couldn't talk looking directly at him. He was not very approachable.

I told Dr. Sam my concerns, and his exact words to me were "So what do you want me to do?"

I was shocked. I felt humiliated and thought maybe I was in the wrong place. Have you ever sweated in an air-conditioned room before? That was me that day. I was choking on tears and felt unwanted and unwelcome. I felt like a slap had hit my face.

I looked halfway at Dr. Sam and said, "I am here for help and to seek your expertise concerning this dilemma." I was choking and breaking the words out in bits and pieces as I managed so hard to speak and, at the same time, control my emotions and tears. Obviously, Dr. Sam did not show any concern. I bet he could care less. I was not the first, and I wouldn't be the last of the number of patients he attended to with similar or worse conditions, I thought. Oh, his demeanor was beyond explanation.

I did not feel welcome at all right from when I walked into the reception area. I get it; sometimes, people may be having a bad day. But my curiosity was three employees at the same location had interacted with me, and the customer-service experience was unacceptable and beyond imagination. That gave me some food for thought.

This was my body in question, so I felt very nervous thinking of the fact that how I could allow this doctor and his entourage to touch my body, my spine, without causing more damage. I felt like I was in the wrong place and started praying fervently, asking God to direct my path in this predicament that I found myself in. I remembered James 1:5, "If any of you lacks wisdom, you should ask God, who gives generously to all without finding fault, and it will be given to you."

Dr. Sam said he would order an MRI report, and I said "great" and thanked him but still allowed God to take over the situation. At least that was one encouraging statement I had heard so far since I walked in here. He said the nurse would be right with me, and that was the last time I saw Dr. Sam even though I went to the office three times.

The nurse I spoke with before Dr. Sam came back in and said prescriptions would be called in to the pharmacy store. I had gotten to a point where I felt like there was no way out of these medications being thrown at me in every shape or form. Pitiful and disgusting. Swallowing pill after pill with zero improvement of healing, but if I missed taking one pill for a few hours, the pain would attack me from every angle. That was the confusing part for me, as the pills were not healing me at all. Who needed that! Very frustrating and challenging.

The MRI report was received at Dr. Sam's office, so I booked another appointment for discussions.

I was ushered into the same room as I had been previously, and a lady walked in with a laptop in her hand, and till this day, I don't believe she ever mentioned her name. She went over the MRI report, and the findings confirmed that I had multiple bulging disks; with numerous readings and explanations of numbers and letters, and the nurse advised that Dr. Sam would have to inject some epidural steroid injection into my lower spine.

The findings in the MRI reports reminded me of Dr. Johnson, at Agape Emergency Room, who had mentioned sciatica in the report he provided to Health First Medical Clinic. He had stated specifically to follow up with a specialist as soon as possible. So why had it taken this long for the referral to the right place in the pursuit of profit at my expense and predicament? That was shameful and not to be wished on anyone.

CHAPTER 10

I received a scheduled date for the epidural-steroid injection procedure in the second week of April 2021. So while waiting, I received a letter from the health-care-insurance provider that the request for the injection had been denied and my doctor had been notified. I was very devastated, and right away, I screenshot the letter and texted it to the number I always received communications from Dr. Sam's office. Somehow, the office phone number was so hard to get through. It didn't feel like an office environment, in my opinion.

I received a response that the office had received the same letter and that a peer-to-peer communication would be done with the health-care-insurance provider.

As the clock was ticking, I was getting worried and kept texting Dr. Sam's office to get any updates on the scheduled procedure approval from the health-care-insurance provider. It felt like pulling teeth just to get the health-care-insurance provider's approval, even though deducting the premiums from one's paycheck was as easy as making a fast buck.

All I was reading was they were working on it, so one day, I called the number that we had been exchanging communications on via text messages, and to my utmost surprise, a woman's voice answered and advised me to go in at the appointed time and date for the injection. So I was so confident and had a sense of hope and relief that everything had been sorted out with no headaches.

A few days after interacting with the woman from Dr. Sam's office, I received a call from that same office, advising me that for the health-care-insurance provider to approve the epidural steroid injection, I had to have another session of physical therapy and a form filled out for evaluation by the physical therapist to prove my inability with the exercises assigned.

I felt very flabbergasted but went ahead and scheduled an appointment for a third session as I thought, since I hadn't done the exercises in a while, this time around, the pain would not be too intense.

As always said, "Had I known" came last. The exercises were no different from the ones before, with the same or worse level of tear in my flesh.

I sent a text message to Dr. Sam's office number, pouring out my heart. I wrote this:

> Today had been very challenging. After the physical therapy yesterday, I felt like a knife was cutting through my right thigh and leg. Too much sensation of beating repeatedly in the inner flesh, bone, and marrow. This was not right. I felt desperate, discouraged and abandoned. I didn't have much hope, and tears, which I couldn't control, were pouring down my cheeks.

Enough was enough! A response came in:

> We are sorry to hear that you are in such pain. If you are unable to continue Physical Therapy, you are not required to do so. We will document this at your next visit and that will suffice for insurance purposes if Physical Therapy is needed to approve anything.

So it came as a surprise when I got another phone call one morning from Dr. Sam's office and the woman on the other end asked how many sessions of physical therapy I had performed.

"Ms. Anderson, the health-care-insurance provider needs to find out how many sessions of physical therapy you did before any approval decision can be made for the upcoming epidural steroid injection. At least there has to be four sessions if need be."

Wow, that blew my mind. I felt like I was getting contradictory information, so I said, "Ma'am, so after the third session of physical therapy that had worsened the pain, you mean the health-care-insurance provider wants me to suffer more unbearable torture, and I mean more damage of my nerves and flesh before they would make a decision concerning my ordeal. That was sad to hear." I said to the woman on the other end of the call, "Tell the health-care-insurance provider that I would not go through another session. Maybe they don't understand, or maybe they just don't care. It's okay to pay all the monthly premiums, but when you need them the most, they find ways and reasons to deny your claim." The woman at the other end of the call responded, "I agree and totally understand your frustration," and we ended the call.

A few days later, I texted Dr. Sam's office number to find out the status with the health-care-insurance provider, and the response I got again was to go in on the appointment date and time.

As I lay flat on my stomach to get some relief from the pain, my inner voice visited me, and what I could hear was "Be strong, and again I say, be strong. You're a woman of substance. Challenging things have happened to you before, but you were never broken nor shaken. You've walked through the valley of the shadow of death before, but you feared no evil. For God has always been with you. His rod and His staff comfort you. You shall get through this too."

I felt like I was reading this psalm as I looked up the ceiling:

> I lift up my eyes to the mountains—where
> does my help come from? My help comes from
> the LORD, the Maker of heaven and earth. He
> will not let your foot slip—he who watches over
> you will not slumber. (Psalms 121:1–3 NIV)

As walking on my feet had started being a challenge, I decided to order a walking cane for additional support. The walking cane was very beautiful, and as I started adjusting to my new norm, it literally became my new companion, whom I named Ms. Diva.

CHAPTER 11

One morning before my scheduled appointment date with Dr. Sam, which was about a week away, I was in so much cruel, pinching pain, so I texted Dr. Sam's office to let him know. It had now become a norm that they barely answered the office phone. I got a response to go in for an evaluation and discuss medication changes if the current ones were not effective, which I had complained about many times, but nothing had been done. Here we go again! Trial and error of medications. It was pathetic! I responded that this had been ongoing: so many medications, and none had reduced the pain for even a whole day.

The person responded, showing concern about how I felt. I texted back that I would go in. As I mentioned before, Dr. Sam's office was just a stone's throw away, so I got in the car and drove slowly there. As I pulled to open the front door, it was locked. I thought that was weird.

I saw a woman walking toward me from inside, and she said, "Can I help you?"

"Yes, ma'am, I am here to see Dr. Sam," I answered.

"Oh, they are not here today, they are at the other office."

Looking perplexed, I said, "This is the only office I know, and I texted the office phone number not long ago, and I received a response to come over."

She responded, "I am sorry, but they're here on Mondays only. I can give you their other location's address, if you would like."

I said, "It's not your fault, but thank you, and I even didn't know they had another office."

I texted Dr. Sam's office about the inconvenience and how challenging it would be to drive about thirty minutes to the other office location. Right away, a response came in, with an apology explaining that they thought I wanted to schedule an appointment for the next Monday at the location close to my house. What?

I was taken aback because I had stated in my initial text message the unmerciful pain that I was experiencing again and again, so why would I want to go in almost a week away? The office sent another text message to ask if I wanted to go to the other office location. As I couldn't take a cab or Uber due to a financial crisis, I struggled to drive slowly almost forty minutes, with rush-hour traffic and lots of frustrations. I arrived and was checked in. There was no verbal apology from the lady at the reception desk even though I expressed my concerns of going that far.

This was difficult to fathom, how professionals behaved this way at Dr. Sam's office. Very despicable behavior and environment. Empathy goes a long way, but that wasn't a vocabulary at Dr. Sam's office most often, I thought.

Dr. Edward administered a steroid injection, which was helpful for five days. I was thankful for the relief and prayed that I would be pain-free from then on.

After the five days, reality set in again. I was tearful and totally lost. The agonizing hell of pain was attacking me all over, as harrowing and as awful as could be. This time it was worse than I could bear. I had heart palpitations. I lay down on the bed and put a pillow over my head. Miraculously, I fell asleep.

As soon as I woke up, I revisited my inner voice, spirit, mind, and soul. In my therapeutic, quiet moments, I read Exodus 15:2 (NIV): "The LORD is my strength and my defense; he has become my salvation. He is my God, and I will praise him, my father's God, and I will exalt him."

I reassured myself that no matter the atrocities haunting me now, it shall all pass away.

I remembered my companion, Ms. Diva, which I had tucked away because I thought I wouldn't need it again for support walking. Good old Ms. Diva and I were walking together again.

CHAPTER 12

Second week of April 2021 was fast approaching, and I was ready for the procedure of the epidural steroid injection. My friend Ebony picked me up on that Monday of the procedure, as I had to have someone to accompany me. On this fateful day, the pain was at its worst. It always happened that way. As always, I had to lie at the back of Ebony's SUV whenever she had to offer me a ride for different reasons. Some good and faithful friends are not easy to find, and I didn't take her services for granted at all. Grateful!

I greeted the receptionist at Dr. Sam's office and handed her my appointment paperwork. She asked for my date of birth and seemed to be searching for a while. She asked for my date of birth again, and I repeated it back to her.

After a few minutes, she said, "Ms. Anderson, I am afraid you don't have an appointment today."

Stunned, I asked her, "Miss, how do you mean I don't have an appointment today when the paperwork clearly states the time and date?"

"That is the appointment paperwork your office gave me, so obviously, something is not adding up."

The receptionist said "Let me research further, Ms. Anderson" as she opened her eyes wide with a serious look on her face, typing so fast, I would think it was about eighty words per minute. She was very proficient. While the receptionist was still researching, my thoughts gathered what had transpired between whoever had been communicating from Dr. Sam's office back and forth via text messages and the call I received about hurting myself more through physical therapy to get an approval from the health-care-insurance provider. But these were secondary thoughts because I had been advised to go in on the said appointment date and time. I had provided enough information to verify my identity so what was the holdup all about?

Ebony was looking at me and vice versa. This was getting very embarrassing especially when other patients were in the waiting area and might have been thinking I didn't have health insurance at all. I was getting agitated because the throbbing and stabbing pain was attacking me crucially as I held on tight to Ms. Diva for support.

After a while, the receptionist said again, "You don't have an appointment, and I can schedule one for you." I said, "I heard you the first time, miss, but you haven't explained to me the reason why I don't have an appointment, when no one at the office called or texted to let me know the appointment had been canceled and not to waste my time coming in only to face this embarrassment."

I was getting frustrated because it had been since February 2021 until April 2021 that I was going through an excruciating, burning, unnecessary ordeal—except for five days of relief, when all the medications I had been swallowing like bitter candy and hated so much with a passion, but I had no choice even though all the relief I got was a 1 out of level 10.

Somebody had to explain to me what was going on. Then the receptionist said, "Oh, Ms. Anderson, I found the reason. It looks like the health-care-insurance provider denied the request, and I would have to reschedule your appointment."

"You got to be kidding me, right?" Other patients, including Ebony, were looking at me, and it was very humiliating.

I said to the receptionist, "If you would excuse me," as I walked away from the counter window, with tears flowing down my cheeks and me holding on to Ms. Diva so tightly for all the support I could count on, because the shocking news had triggered the pain more and I was shaking tremendously.

My first instinct was to step outside the office and call the health-care-insurance provider to find out what was going on.

Nancy was pleasant at the other end, and I recalled trying so hard to hold back the tears as I was telling Nancy my experience at Dr. Sam's office. Nancy showed a lot of empathy and said, "Ms.

Anderson, the request by Dr. Sam was approved, so let me place you on a brief hold and call his office right away. I am sincerely sorry you had to go through this. Nobody deserves to be treated this way." Those soothing words from Nancy made me so emotional, but the outpouring of tears turned into tears of joy and relief. At least someone cared.

After putting me on hold for about four minutes, Nancy connected back with me and said, "Ms. Anderson, just to let you know I am still waiting to speak to someone at the office, there is just a recording playing over and over. I will place you on hold again. I am so sorry for the inconvenience." Nancy connected back to me after about ten minutes and said no one answered the phone, which didn't surprise me at all. I told Nancy about the bad experiences I had encountered at Dr. Sam's office, and I requested for her to find me another pain-management specialist right away. Sigh! Wasted months, weeks, and days! But God works in mysterious ways. There had been lots and lots of red flags at this office. God always reveals to redeem. This, to me, was a delicate procedure, and anything could have gone wrong when one was dealing with such irresponsible professionals in the medical field. That was very unsettling.

My inner spirit was down. I didn't wish this experience on anyone. Ever! But that peace of tranquility returned to my senses, and all I wanted to do was to go back home and lie flat on my stomach to get all the strength and relief from the nagging torture. Ebony spent some time with me and reassured me that all would be well. It was just a matter of time.

Before long on that same day, Dr. Wangi had become my new pain-management specialist.

After resting and rejuvenated from the dilemma at Dr. Sam's office, I drove slowly to the Spine Care Clinic of Dr. Wangi's office without an appointment.

The young lady at the receptionist welcomed me as I walked in to show them all the paperwork I collected from Dr. Sam's office. With a wide smile on the receptionist's face, she asked if I had an appointment. I said no and told them what had transpired. Obviously, I could see the three ladies faces of astonishment, even though the staff didn't say anything to break their oath of medical professionalism, I would think. Angela at Dr. Wangi's office set up an appointment date for me that same week. My first visit was very welcoming, and at this time, all necessary paperwork had been transferred from my health-care-insurance provider to Dr. Wangi's office within a twinkle of an eye. Impressive!

In the last week of April 2021, I was scheduled for the epidural steroid injection on my next appointment date.

Dr Wangi's assistant, James, greeted me on the day of the procedure and went over the whole process with me. James was pleasant to talk to, made me feel welcome, and assured me that all would be well. "Do you have any questions, Ms. Anderson, before Dr. Wangi comes in?" James asked. I surely did. "So how long does the whole procedure take, and I am sure this would get me on my feet without the pain again very soon, right?" I asked.

"The procedure takes about thirty minutes, and the injection would be in your body for about six months to one year."

That got me startled. "Hmmm, I thought this injection was used to eradicate the issue forever?" I asked.

James said, if after six months or after one year the injection wears out in the spine, they would inject a booster.

I was not very enthused about that information, but we would see how that went. With much praying, I hoped that this was the end of the torturing pain and a new beginning.

I had the option to have the injection with or without an anesthesia, and I objected the anesthesia.

Dr. Wangi walked in and greeted me with a smile. I wasn't surprised about all the exceptional reviews that I read online about him and his staff. That put my mind at peace.

After some interactions on how the whole procedure worked, of which James had already discussed most of with me, we were ready to start.

The whole procedure was uncomfortable and hurt from time to time, and it made sense why an anesthesia would be recommended.

Well, if you had given birth naturally or had the torment I had been experiencing for all these months, then I would say the injections were nothing close to the former and the latter.

We were done in no time, and a follow-up appointment was scheduled.

At least Ms. Diva, my walking cane, would have some rest; that was what I thought.

After Healing

CHAPTER 13

Day 4 after the injections, and I was still in my worst moments of pain, more than I could ever handle. It didn't add up at all. I emailed Dr. Wangi's office to let him know of my condition and concerns. The office staff were very prompt to respond to emails or return phone calls. Anita called to advise me that the epidural steroid injection would start taking effect from five to ten days. I guess I didn't know that, and as the old adage goes, patience always moves mountains.

I went back to good old Ms. Diva for walking support.

After day 15, I was not close to getting a relief. That bothered me. I also noticed that when I stood on my feet for about an hour, my right foot would start to swell like the size of a small blown balloon. I was scared to look at my own foot. One time, my right foot was so swollen I had to email a picture to Dr. Wangi.

Dr. Wangi discussed with me that since the epidural steroid injection had not relieved the pain, he had to repeat the injection with a focus on more trigger points in the spine, so the second week in May 2021, I was scheduled for the procedure. Obviously, I was not a happy camper.

I was feeling very nervous, as uncertainties of the unknown set in. Ironically, the pain level was getting worse and worse than I could ever imagine. The injections had not alleviated the internal snapping sensations of the right thigh and right leg but became a rather more burning, throbbing, swollen foot, uncomfortable pinching, way worse than before.

The tears and agony had become too much to bear. Some days, I would look at my face in the mirror and ask myself over and over, when shall all this be over? It was just a matter of time, but I was getting tired and frustrated, but then Jeremiah 32:27 reminded me of who God still is, "Behold, I am the Lord, the God of all flesh: is there anything too hard for me?"

That was so true. I was only human, but I will have the peace of stillness and know that God is still on the throne. It's such a powerful statement of truth. I read these words from a songwriter, and the words really calmed me down whenever I couldn't bear the pain.

"I don't want to be afraid, every time I face the waves. I don't want to fear the storm just because I hear it roar. Peace be still. Say the word and I will set my feet upon the sea. Till I'm dancing in the deep. You are here so it is well. Even when my eyes can't see. I will trust the voice that speaks."

Listening to the words of the song was so soothing and promising to brighten my day.

I started praying these words; I lifted up my eyes to the hills—where does my help come from? My help comes from the Lord, the Maker of heaven and earth. Indeed, He who watches over Israel will neither slumber nor sleep. The sun will not harm you by day, nor the moon by night.

With that peace and consolation of joy like a river in my heart, I fell asleep.

The next morning as I walked into Dr. Wangi's office, I was greeted as always with a beautiful smile by the receptionist. I again declined the anesthesia as there was fees involved and with expenses high but less income to foot the bills; I had to protect every nickel and dime I had left. I thought, once I had endured the first injection without the anesthesia, I would be okay for the second injection.

Not long after Dr. Wangi started the procedure, I knew right away I should have had the anesthesia. It was intense, fast and furious, and hurt more than the first injection did as this took longer.

Back home and lying on the floor, which had become my comfort zone of rest, I started thinking deeply. I was scared. My confidence level was not where it needed to be. All because the first injection did not alleviate the pain, and now a second one. What was the guarantee that this one would work? I said to myself, I had come this far by faith, leaning on God's words and promises, so I was confident yet shaken that the results would be positive.

Maybe I was just anxious, but God tells us not to be anxious about anything, so that was the confidence I had.

Day 5 turned to day 10, and as my doubts had been settling in, the pain level was at its worst. I was devastated. How come none of the injections were effective? The pros versus the cons sounded promising, so how come I did not experience the slightest relief? Oh, goodness!

I emailed Dr. Wangi's office to let him know about my current condition, which hadn't been different from before. I was very discouraged and frustrated.

As the epidural steroid injection had been injected twice, Dr. Wangi advised and recommended a referral to a surgeon for expert counselling and further evaluation. Tell me we hadn't come this far for nothing, and now I had to see a surgeon? My eyes couldn't control the tears that were pouring down my cheeks like hail falling from the skies.

So this journey started with going to Agape Emergency Room, then a referral to Health First Medical Clinic, where two X-rays reported no issues to be concerned about, except mild arthritis in the right thigh, medications upon medications, as they didn't adhere to Dr. Johnson's recommendations to see a specialist as soon as possible. Then referral to Wellness Physical Therapy, which was unimaginably hurtful. Then referral to Dr. Sam, which didn't go too well, so another referral to Dr. Wangi, and now a referral to a surgeon. It had seriously been a journey of unmerciful pain and torture. Very heartbreaking.

CHAPTER 14

As soon as my appointment was booked with Dr. Wiley, I went online to Google his reviews. It was quite impressive that over 250 reviews would all have a five-star rating. That gave me some sense of reassurance.

I was welcomed at Perfect Spine Specialists Clinic, and the receptionist at the desk had a very captivating smile. Melissa introduced herself and had all paperwork ready for me as I filled them online. It was an easy process, and within about ten minutes, I was ushered in to meet Dr. Wiley. Even though he had his mask on, his saying of "Hello, Ms. Anderson" was clear and vibrant, and we did the elbow greeting, which I thought was very welcoming. He gave me a lot of information; we went over my MRI and X-ray reports together. We watched a video of the procedure he advised, and he recommended that would eliminate the stabbing and antagonizing pain. To tell you the truth, this had been the first doctor I had seen in years who was very thorough. He went above and beyond. Maybe that's what spine surgeons do. This experience was phenomenal! It compared to none.

A few days after meeting with Dr. Wiley, his nurse coordinator, Sarah, called to schedule a date for the upcoming procedure, as well as presurgery blood lab tests, X-ray, EKG, urine, et cetera.

My eyes brightened up like those of a little kid whose parents went home with a big surprise for him. I started to breathe with joy in my soul, mind, and spirit, thinking of the fact that I missed sitting on a chair to eat like a normal human being would, sleeping comfortably on a bed, which I did every now and then, but it wasn't the same. I missed standing or walking for long periods without feeling pain or a swollen foot afterward. I missed driving myself and doing things on my own time, sitting comfortably on the toilet seat, and not having to cry like a child looking for his favorite toy.

The second week of July was my early-morning surgery day. It was a beautiful, calm morning, and I couldn't be happier as my sister Sonia came to pick me up, heading to We Care Spine Hospital, which was the main hospital where all the surgeons worked. We had an amazing conversation about a lot of things except the upcoming surgery. I guess it was to put my mind at peace and inwardly reassure me that everything would be okay. God had already conquered the battle, and the rest was just to celebrate His goodness and mercy upon our lives.

We arrived an hour early as it has been a habit forming over the years. I hate tardiness unless it is necessary.

All the two nurse assistants in the waiting area were very upbeat, wishing everyone all the best. The whole atmosphere was serene, and that made me forget what was ahead of me. Apart from the staff being professional, we all felt like one big, happy family. The awards that surrounded the hospital's waiting area from year after year were proven records of what these surgeons were capable of doing.

CHAPTER 15

I was ushered into the curtained prep room for surgery. Mary, one of the nurses in charge, was good at heart inside and out. She had a calm way of communicating, and I could tell she did that with every patient. Mary rechecked my name on the wristband (put on at the waiting area), date of birth, as well as what type of procedure I was in for. She put on my bed some stuff that she would need to have all set up for me to be wheeled away to the operating room, once the anesthesia doctor came in to give directions. All crew members had to be in sync with one another, and it was interesting and important to watch how they coordinated with one another while dealing with human lives. While I was daydreaming and feeling the warmth of the hot blanket over my body, Mary came in with a list of the medications I had been taking, to go over them with me. I took the plastic bottles of medications I brought from home to compare.

One of the names of medications Mary mentioned did not ring a bell. "Mary, I don't take Celebrex," I said. "Well, it's on the printed sheet I have, let me see your medications bottles. Oh, you do take celecoxib, which is a generic name for Celebrex. I will be right back, Ms. Anderson," Mary said.

Casting my mind back to a few weeks before the surgery, Sarah from Dr. Wiley's office had left a voice message, as well as emailed me a presurgery instructions of the dos and don'ts. On the list of medications not to take, among others, was Celebrex, so as I checked with my medications list at home, I said to myself I was all cleared. I didn't take any of those medications listed.

Not knowing the seriousness of the impact this was going to have on me having the surgery, I lay calmly on my bed and started communicating with my inner mind that this was it. I was ready to say goodbye to the pain that had haunted and tortured me like a double-edged sword, piercing through my joints and marrow for months. I felt so much joy like a river in my soul.

Mary walked in and asked, "Ms. Anderson, when was the last time you took the celecoxib?" Somehow my heart skipped a beat. I answered, "At 8:30 p.m. last night. Is everything okay?" As curiosity killed the cat, I said to myself, I was ready to know what was going on. Mary said she would be right back and left the room.

In about fifteen minutes, Mary returned and said, "Ms. Anderson, I am afraid we cannot do the surgery today, please get dressed, and Dr. Wiley would come and talk to you in the waiting area."

I felt like my life had come to an end. I was shattered. My curiosity had come to light, and I guess it was not her call to explain and answer the why that was raging through my mind. For a moment I rebuked that spirit of anger over me and started saying, "God, Thou will be done. And in all circumstances, whether good or bad, I shall still praise Your holy name."

As I sat in the waiting area, two men working at the hospital asked if I needed some warm blankets. I guess, if nothing at all, I had to enjoy the warmth of these blankets before I left. Either way, surgery or no surgery, I believe the hospital would still bill me for those services.

Dr. Wiley came in and, as always, with a vibrant smile and a positive attitude that was so contagious, greeted and started explaining some things to me.

"Well, Ms. Anderson, it looks like we would have to reschedule your surgery because the Celebrex, which has a generic name as celecoxib, is a blood thinner, and we cannot take chances for possible bleeding after surgery. Abigail, the nurse coordinator, would call to set up a new date for the surgery."

"I am a bit disappointed, Dr. Wiley, but I know it's not your fault. Thank you, and I look forward to my next appointment date," I said.

CHAPTER 16

Patricia, the nurse practitioner, excused me from work while recuperating from the pain. Has anyone experienced how so many thoughts overflow their mind as they recuperate from an illness? I bet the answer is yes, but my thoughts were in a different dimension. I started thinking of the visit to Agape Emergency Room and what Dr. Johnson had said would be the root cause of this godforsaken, nerve-racking ordeal.

So why was Patricia not in sync with Dr. Johnson as far as the diagnosis went? It kept bothering me.

After several days of me taking the numerous medications, Patricia requested for some X-rays of the hip, for which I was advised that the readings showed mild arthritis. Another X-ray that was requested for the femur didn't show any issues to be concerned about.

As I was thinking back, my memory reconnected to when I had my appointment with Patricia at Health First Medical Clinic back in February 2021; the medication celecoxib, among others, was prescribed for the pain. I had been taking it since. My X-ray report showed mild arthritis, from what Patricia had discussed with me, and she didn't think that was the root cause of the pain I was experiencing.

So now to think back, why had I been taking the medication for over five months without Patricia or Dr. Sam advising me to stop, as I had been taking the medication for the wrong reason? Was there some kind of incentive from the pharmaceutical industries to the doctors, for the more godforsaken pills a patient swallowed? That really bothered me. This was my life at risk here.

Because these medications were prescribed by Patricia, Dr. Sam, and Dr. Wangi, some had become autorefills while others had to get authorization from the health-care-insurance providers after a urine test. So if Dr. Wiley and Mary had not brought up this blood thinner associated with the celecoxib also known as Celebrex, I would have maybe taken this medication forever.

Patricia had prescribed the celecoxib, and when Dr. Sam took over my medical chart, he submitted to the pharmacy department Celebrex when I ran low, which was in fine print on the medication bottle, after looking closely at all the jargon of words written on the bottle. That was where the confusion was.

A new date for the surgery was scheduled, at the end of July 2021.

While waiting for the new surgery date, I sent a text message to Dr. Sam's office, asking when I would be taking off some of the medications, as the surgery date was approaching fast, and the response was, so long as they were not giving me any side effects, I had to continue taking them. That bothered me because at what point did you even know that medications were affecting any organs in your body, when you got such a response? I am not an expert in the medical field, but obviously, I was curious in my specific situation and predicament as to why no blood work was even done to examine the extent of the medication's side effects.

One day, I went to check the mailbox, and there was a mail from Agape Emergency Room. I wasn't surprised and thought it might be a small leftover bill from the health-care-insurance provider. It was a statement showing all the breakdown charges. For a less-than-two-hour visit, there was a bill of $5,100 rounded up, billed to the health-care-insurance provider. The insurance company paid $3,400 rounded up, and the rest was billed to me. The $500 I paid before services rendered was included in the statement. I was confused. I was injected a shot of steroid injection that did not work and a prescription to be picked up at the pharmacy store, and I got billed this much?

CHAPTER 17

The D-day had finally arrived for the procedure to be done. After my checking in and getting a bed assigned, Peter came in and went over all the paperwork, as usual. Oh, thank God I was all cleared this time with nothing to worry about. It felt like Christmas in July! Peter's team were one of the most amazing people to come across. I had literally gotten a new family before I was wheeled away to the operating room. We talked about different countries in the world, their cultures, and the amazing people we come across that made a difference in other people's lives.

Then Isaac and Naomi came in for the anesthesia process but couldn't help joining in to the conversation. Saying goodbye to my new family was heartbreaking, but I now had to focus on the reason for going in.

I heard someone call out my name, but I was in a different world as the voice I was hearing sounded far away. Then it felt like I was dreaming, but I couldn't remember the dream. Oh, surgery was over, and I was in the recovery room. Funny how I had no clue when I was put to sleep and how long the surgery took.

Praises to God as I came out of the slumber successfully, discharged and ready to go home. On day 3 after surgery, I had already sat down comfortably on a chair to enjoy a meal.

I had an appointment with Dr. Wiley two weeks after the surgery, and he couldn't praise me enough for taking care of the wound at my lower back, where the surgery was performed. He said it had healed very well. We discussed my overall wellness after surgery, and I was glad to give a nine-out-of-ten rating for the first time in over six months.

The nerves that had experienced lots and lots of trauma over the months were healing slowly, but overall, I was very thankful and grateful to this amazing and phenomenal doctor God ordained to take over my case and helped me tremendously on the road to recovery!

Dr. Wiley advised that the nerves would take some time to heal and to take it one day at a time.

From time to time, the nerves would hurt, but nothing compared to previous burning sensations and throbbing pains. The road to recovery seemed to be coming along very well, and I was forever grateful. What shall I render unto the Lord for His goodness, grace, mercy and protection?

Now both doctors Wiley and Wangi were working pari passu with different scheduled appointments for follow-ups with the highest focus on the nerves, as there had been lots of trauma over the past months while waiting in vain for so many decisions to be made, hence an extensive damage of the nerves but treatable. In the meantime, another physical-therapy clinic by the name Blissful Physical Therapy had been scheduled for me, and the ratings online were exceptional.

My visit to Blissful Physical Therapy was an amazing experience of new beginnings. Stephanie was thorough about every detailed information we needed to go over. She was so easy to talk to and assured me that the painful experiences before at Wellness Physical Therapy were a thing of the past. True to her word, my sessions had been one of the best experiences to be proud of.

I still had some restrictions as it was important to take things one day at a time, but so far, the road ahead looks very promising. There has been a wide smile on my face.

I felt so relieved that I didn't have to be at the mercy of all these medications that were not effective 98 percent of the time. There are only two medications now, of which one is for the nerves, and the other only as needed for pain or spasm, which, thankfully, I have not taken in weeks.

In ending my ordeal, which lasted 169 days of chronic, excruciating, burning, throbbing, pinching, piercing torture before surgery, I went from "the unmerciful pain," to merciful grace from God that surpasses all understanding.

First Time in Church

ABOUT THE AUTHOR

Madison Esther Panti, affectionately called Maddy by family members and friends, originated from Ghana, in West Africa. After graduating second-year college in Ghana, she went straight to the workforce into banking. She married at a tender age and bore a daughter, who has been a blessing over the years. She migrated to the USA to pursue her passion in the banking industry, graduated from Caliber Training Institute in New York, New York. With her hard work and dedication, she was promoted to branch supervisor in New York and branch manager in Dallas, Texas, respectively. She currently lives in San Antonio, Texas, and is still in the banking industry at the corporate office of one of the largest banks in the world.